Life in the American Colonies

The Dish on FOOD and FARMING in Colonial America

by Anika Fajardo

Consultant:
Dr. Samuel B. Hoff
Professor of History
Delaware State University
Dover, Delaware

CAPSTONE PRESS
a capstone imprint

Fact Finders are published by Capstone Press,
151 Good Counsel Drive, P.O. Box 669, Mankato, Minnesota 56002.
www.capstonepub.com

Library of Congress Cataloging-in-Publication Data
Fajardo, Anika.
The dish on food and farming in colonial America / by Anika Fajardo.
 p. cm.—(Fact finders. Life in the American colonies.)
 Includes bibliographical references and index.
ISBN 978-1-4296-6492-9 (library binding)
ISBN 978-1-4296-7217-7 (paperback)
 1. Food habits—United States—History—Juvenile literature. 2. Agriculture—United States—
History—Juvenile literature. 3. United States—History—Colonial period, ca. 1600–1775—Juvenile
literature. 4. United States—Social life and customs—To 1775—Juvenile literature. I. Title.
 GT2853.U5F35 2012
 394.1'20973—dc22   2011002117

Editorial Credits
Jennifer Besel, editor; Ashlee Suker, designer; Wanda Winch, media researcher;
    Eric Manske, production specialist

Photo Credits
Alamy: Nathan Benn, 28, North Wind Picture Archives, 8, 16, 18, 20, Pictorial Press Ltd, 19; The
Bridgeman Art Library International: Peter Newark American Pictures, 15, 26; Corbis: Reuters/
Jim Young, 23, Richard T. Nowitz, 10; Dorrie Williams, 9; iStockphoto: Bronwyn8, 21; The Library of
Virginia, 25; National Parks Service: Colonial National Historical Park/Sidney E. King, artist, 6, 7, 12,
24; North Wind Picture Archives, cover; Shutterstock: alexkar08, linen strip design, Anna Ozerina, floral
background, Irina Tischenko, charred wood design, Michael Vigliotti, 14, Morgan Lane Photography, 17,
Oleg Kozlov, 22, photocell, frame design, Viachaslau Kraskouski, wooden floor design

Printed in the United States of America in Stevens Point, Wisconsin.
032011   006111WZF11

TABLE OF CONTENTS

PEOPLE
of the COLONIES

For people in the American colonies, getting enough food was a daily struggle. Grocery stores and restaurants did not exist. During the colonial period (1607–1776), people had to hunt, grow, find, and prepare everything they ate.

The groups of people who lived in the American colonies had to develop ways to feed themselves. Indian tribes had lived in America for hundreds of years. They developed farming techniques that worked in America's **climates**. They also became skilled hunters.

The early colonists were mostly wealthy men and women. They were used to living in warm homes where food was plentiful. They had no idea how to farm or hunt for food. They learned much from the American Indians on how to survive in the wild land.

climate—the usual weather in a place

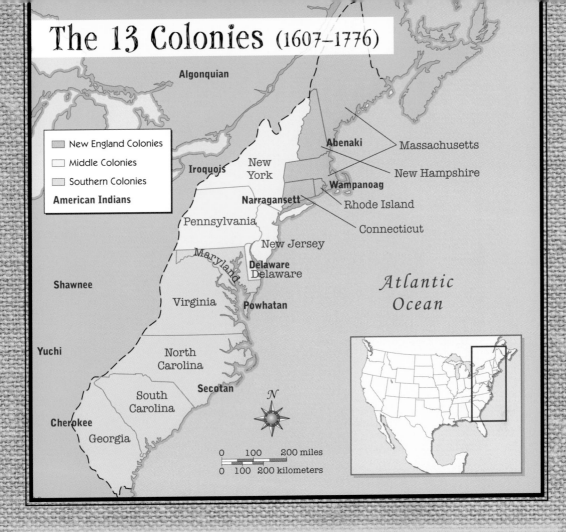

The 13 Colonies (1607–1776)

Algonquian

New England Colonies
Middle Colonies
Southern Colonies
American Indians

Abenaki — Massachusetts

Iroquois — New York — New Hampshire

Wampanoag

Narragansett — Rhode Island

Pennsylvania — Connecticut

New Jersey

Maryland — Delaware Delaware

Shawnee

Virginia — Powhatan

Atlantic Ocean

Yuchi

North Carolina

Secotan

South Carolina

Cherokee

Georgia

N

0   100   200 miles
0   100   200 kilometers

Colonists brought slaves and servants to the colonies. These people worked on farms, growing the colonists' crops. Growing, preparing, and **preserving** food was a major part of each person's day. Everyone—men, women, and children—had to work if they wanted to eat.

preserve—to treat food so it does not spoil

Chapter 1

Learning to SURVIVE

Jamestown colonists came looking for gold and other treasures.

When Europeans arrived in the New World in the 1600s, they brought barrels of food with them. But they didn't have a plan for when the barrels ran dry. Instead, their thoughts were on the riches they hoped to find.

Colonists settled Jamestown, Virginia, in 1607. Instead of farming, most searched for gold and other riches. But there were none. By the winter of 1609–1610, the colonists had used up their food supplies. They had not grown enough crops to last the rough winter. The men were dying of starvation. Desperate, they began to eat the flesh of those who had died.

After that terrible winter, the colonists understood the importance of hunting, farming, and preserving food. They realized the American Indians had a wealth of knowledge and could teach them how to survive.

The first colonists built huts to live in, but they didn't grow enough food for winter.

INDIAN CORN

Corn, or maize, was the main food for American Indians in the northeast. Maize wasn't sweet like the corn on the cob we eat today. And it wasn't always yellow. The kernels could be orange, red, or brown. After **harvesting**, maize had to be ground into corn meal. Women used a tool called a mortar and pestle to grind the kernels. The corn meal was then used to make corn bread and many other dishes.

American Indians learned to grow and use maize long before colonists arrived.

Before coming to America, colonists had never seen corn. But it soon became a main part of their diets. The American Indians taught the colonists how to grow and use corn. The colonists began calling the crop "Indian corn," and they used it in almost every meal.

American Indians also introduced colonists to pumpkins. They taught them to roast pumpkins in a fire or dry them like jerky.

a mortar and pestle with corn

Chapter 2

MEALTIME

The biggest meal for colonists was dinner. This meal was served in the middle of the day. For most white colonists, dinner almost always included meat, usually pork. European colonists brought pigs to the New World. Soon pigs waddled all over farmyards, Indian villages, and wealthy estates. One colonist said people ate so much pork they were beginning to grunt instead of speak.

Dinner wasn't the same for all colonists though. The food served at dinner depended on how wealthy the people were. Poorer families ate thick stews of pork, cabbage, and corn. The stew was served on a piece of stale bread.

a re-enactment of meal preparation in colonial times

Colonists ate the brains, skin, tails, and blood of pigs.

Slaves were fed **rations** of corn and pork. They cooked corn "hoe cakes" over a fire on the end of a hoe. They ate parts of the pig no one wanted, such as the ears, feet, and ribs.

Rich families usually ate two courses at dinner. The first course included soups, meat puddings, and meat pies. For some families, dinner also included vegetables cooked into a soft sauce.

When fruit and sugar were available, the second course was dessert. Pastries, puddings, and dumplings were made with fruits, such as cherries, mulberries, plums, and apples.

ration—a limited amount of something

BREAKFAST AND SUPPER

Breakfast and supper were served only if there was enough food. After morning chores, colonists would eat a steaming bowl of porridge made with maize. Porridge was a bit like oatmeal.

Most colonists didn't eat supper. If they did, it was leftovers. They might have homemade bread and butter and more porridge. The porridge at supper might include a bit of bacon or deer meat.

Colonists pressed fruits, such as grapes, to make their own wine.

BEVERAGES

Colonists didn't drink much water. Some of the water from lakes and streams was dirty. It sometimes made people sick. So colonists had **alcoholic** drinks instead. Everyone drank beer and wine—even children. The colonists made beer from grains such as corn. They made wine from fruit.

Colonists also drank tea. Black tea was **imported** from China and India. The colonists thought tea was both fashionable and delicious. By the end of the colonial period, tea was a favorite drink for colonists. The American Indians also drank tea. They made tea from plants that grew in the area.

alcoholic—containing alcohol

import—to bring goods into one country from another

Chapter 3

HUNTING and FARMING

People who wanted meat for dinner had to hunt. And they weren't picky about which animals they would eat. Wild turkeys, fish, and rabbits made good meals. So did pigeons, turtles, and raccoons. But the favorite was **venison**.

The European colonists hunted game with muskets or rifles. But they weren't very good hunters at first. In Europe hunting was a sport men did for fun. The American Indians showed the colonists that hunting could be done to find food.

In most tribes, American Indian men left their villages for days at a time to hunt. They hunted their prey with bows, arrows, and spears. They studied the animals to understand their movements. This knowledge made it easier to find and hunt prey.

an American Indian spear

venison—deer meat

In New England, colonists dried cod to eat in winter.

Fish was also a source of food for colonists and American Indians who lived near water. In New England, clams, lobsters, crabs, and oysters were reliable food sources. In the Hudson River, colonists caught sturgeon and eels for dinner.

FARMING

The American Indians were skilled at planting and harvesting food that grew well in the rich soil near rivers. The men burned grasses and brush to clear the land. Then the women planted the fields. Children helped weed the fields and harvest crops.

The Indians grew three main crops—corn, beans, and squash. They planted corn on little mounds of dirt. Then, between the corn stalks, they planted beans. Bean vines grew up the stalks of corn. Then they planted squash between the rows of corn. The squash helped keep weeds from growing.

an illustration of an American Indian village and gardens in the 1600s

Colonists began to use this clever way of planting. But the colonists also brought many changes to farming. Before the colonists arrived, American Indians farmed with wooden or stone hoes. Colonists brought machinery such as plows from Europe. They also brought cows and horses. For a while, there was actually more livestock than people in the colonies!

Three Sisters

Corn, beans, and squash were not just delicious and nutritious. They were spiritually important to American Indians. These plants were called the Three Sisters. Tribes tell different stories about the Three Sisters. In all of them, the Three Sisters are three very different spirits. Even though they were different, they all worked together. The Indians always planted, ate, and celebrated corn, beans, and squash together.

FARM LABORERS

A mouth to feed also had hands to work. Everyone had to work hard to survive in the colonies. Children shoveled manure. They weeded fields. They walked through scratchy rows of plants to pick corn. Over time, colonial farms grew larger to meet the colonies' growing demand for crops. Farmers needed more help. So the colonists brought in slaves.

White slaves from Europe were called indentured servants. These people traded their freedom for a trip to the New World. Most servants worked on farms in the middle and New England colonies. They didn't own land or have any rights. Some masters beat their servants. But after four to eight years of hard labor, they were set free.

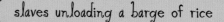

slaves unloading a barge of rice

In the southern colonies, slaves from Africa, the Caribbean Islands, and other places worked on tobacco or rice **plantations**. They worked 16-hour days and lived in crowded little cabins. Slave masters whipped or beat slaves who didn't do as they were told.

Slaves and servants made it possible for farms to grow large amounts of crops. The crops could then be sold to make money.

Slaves were sold at auctions to the highest bidders.

plantation—a large farm found in warm areas

Chapter 4

COOKING and PRESERVING

Cooking over an open fire was dangerous. Burns were common.

Once the food was hunted or harvested, there was still much work to do. It still had to be prepared or preserved. Women took on most of this work.

Stoves hadn't been invented yet, so women cooked over fires. Some cooking fires were outside the house. Others were in large fireplaces in the house. Many colonial women baked in Dutch ovens. These heavy iron pots hung over the fire from large hooks. The cook adjusted the temperature by moving the Dutch oven closer to or farther from the flames. She tested the heat by holding her arm over the fire. The hotter the fire, the shorter time she could hold her arm there.

As colonists grew wealthier, they built larger kitchens with fireplaces. But stray sparks from the fire could be dangerous. For safety they often built kitchens away from the house. In southern plantations, kitchens were often far away from slave cabins too. The owners feared slaves might take food.

Making Butter

Making butter was a hard job for women. First they milked the cows. Then they used cloth to strain dirt, flies, and cow hair out of the milk. They set the milk out in bowls for a couple days. The cream would rise to the top. Then the cream was mixed in a butter churn. Women and girls developed strong muscles as they moved the plunger up and down in the churn. After as long as three hours, the cream turned to butter. Sometimes the women would sing songs while churning. Here is one of the butter songs:

"Come Butter come, Come Butter come, Peter stands at the Gate, Waiting for a buttered Cake, Come Butter come."

STORING FOOD

Mushy, rotten turnips. Gray, fuzzy chunks of meat. These are the signs of spoiled food. Cold winters froze vegetables. Hot summers caused meat to mold. The colonists had to find ways to keep food from spoiling.

The colonists stored vegetables and fruits in root cellars. These underground pits usually kept foods at a constant temperature. But spring rains often flooded cellars, causing the food to rot. And a full cellar was an all-you-can-eat buffet for hungry rats.

Fast Fact

Some colonists wouldn't eat vegetables because they thought veggies were bad for them.

a re-enactment of how colonists hung dried meat from the ceilings of their homes

Colonists used salt to keep meat from spoiling. Men butchered pigs, cows, deer, and other animals. They stored the hunks of meat in large containers filled with salt. The salt kept bacteria from growing and rotting the meat.

Drying also kept meat from rotting. Meat was left to dry in the sun or in the ashes of a dying fire. Then colonists hung the preserved meat from the ceilings of their houses. All winter long, women cut pieces of meat off these slabs for dinner.

Chapter 5

TRADING

A single colonial family couldn't grow or gather everything they needed or wanted. Colonists got what they couldn't make or grow themselves by trading. Early colonists often traded with each other. A man might trade a day of labor for a basket of vegetables to feed his family.

Early colonists traded tools and weapons to American Indians in exchange for food.

Colonists traded with the American Indians too. The Indians had furs and seeds the colonists needed. The colonists had iron pots, guns, and other manufactured goods from Europe. So the two groups often traded.

Over time towns grew out of the American wilderness. **Merchants** imported food and goods from England. They sold their items in general stores. General stores made it easier for people to get food, seeds, and spices.

merchant—a person who buys and sells goods for profit

Greenhow's Store

John Greenhow owned a general store in Williamsburg, Virginia. He sold almost anything colonists might need. All of his goods were from England. The foods he sold included tea, coffee, chocolate, spices, currants, and plums. He also sold household items, such as Dutch ovens and other cooking pots.

SOLD at John Greenhow's *Store, near the Church in Williamsburg, very cheap for ready Money,* LINENS of moſt Sorts, Breadths, and Fineneſs, Durants, Tammies, Sagathies, Stuffs, Everlaſtings, Calicoes, printed Linens, Bed Ticks, faſhionable Mens and Childrens Hats, Hyſon, Congo, Green, and Bohea Teas, *India* Damaſks, white Calico, *India* Dimity and Humhums, all imported before the Aſſociation took Place; Coffee and Chocolate, Pots and Mills for do. Iron and Copper Tea Kettles, Iron Pots of all Sorts and Sizes, Iron *Dutch* Ovens, Salamanders, Dogs and Backs, Skillets, Mortars and Peſtles, Sheet Iron, Tin Sheets, wove Braſs Wire for Riddle Bottoms, *Dutch* Fans and Safes, large, noble, and rich *China* Bowls, and various other Sorts of *China* Ware, Glaſs, Pewter, Tin, Stone, and Delf Ware of moſt Sorts, a large Aſſortment of Looking Glaſſes, Ivory Memorandum Books, a large Aſſortment of Surveyors Inſtruments, either in complete Sets or ſeparate, Chapes and Tongues for Silver Buckles of moſt Sizes, moſt Kinds of Tools and Materials for Carpenters, Silverſmiths, Watchmakers, Blackſmiths, Shoemakers, Bricklayers, and Saddlers, Crucibles, Silverſmiths caſting Sand, prepared Emery, and other poliſhing Powders, Screw Plates and Files of moſt Sorts, Mill Saws, Whip Saws, and moſt other Kinds of Saws, Whalebone, and every other Article for the Staymaking Buſineſs, Stockings, Gloves, Fans, Bugies, Paſte Combs and Combs of all Sorts, Hunting Horns tipped and plain, *German* Flutes and Fifes, Spinnet Wire and Hammers, Teeth Inſtruments and Teeth Drawers of all Sorts; Cryſtals and main Springs for Watches, yellow Canvas and Worſted Shades, Whitechapel Needles, Blunts, Sharps, and Squares, a large Aſſortment of freſh and genuine Drugs and Medicines at an unuſual low Price, Spices of all Sorts, Currants, Plums, Almonds, Candy, Sweetmeats, beſt Sallad Oil, Vinegar, Wines, Rice, Barley, ſplit Peas, Sago, Salop, Clover Seed, Lucern, Rape, Saintfoin, Timothy, *French* Furze, Flax Seed, Linſeed and Train Oil, Paints, Bruſhes, and Pencils of almoſt all Sorts, Shells of Water Colours, a great Variety of Locks of all Sorts common and curious, Nails, Hinges, and moſt Sorts of Materials for building, Window Glaſs, Horſe Collars, Chain Traces, Well Chains, Warming Pans, Coopers Tools, Cart and Chair Wheel Boxes of all Sizes, Iron Wire, Spades and Shovels, Seine Twine and Cork, Copperas, Madder, Redwood, Logwood, Alum, Half Gallon ſquare Caſe Bottles, Iron Weights from one to fifty ſix Pounds, Weights for Money from one Grain to three Ounces, Hour Glaſſes, Pewter Meaſures, Houſe Bells, Barbers weaving Silk and Thread, Toys, Candleſticks, Family Bibles, Prayer Books, Diſpenſatories, Tiſſot and Fothergill on Health, and various other Books and Stationary, Candle Moulds, Fiddles, and *Roman* Fiddle Strings, Sheep and Tailors Shears, Silver Thimbles of all Sizes, Bed Screws, Wool, Cotton, and playing Cards, ſingle and double Bed Blankets, Pumice and rotten Stone, Nipple Glaſſes, Coal and Duſt Shovels and Trivets, Shaving Boxes and Soap, Billiard Balls, Dice and Boxes, Cock Gaffs, Key Rings, Toothpick Caſes, Court Plaiſter, Shoe Irons, Silk Purſes, Rules and Squares, Box and Flat Irons, Fiddleſticks, Beaver and Vermin Traps, Bar Steel of all Sorts, *Moor's* beſt Graſs and Bramble Scythes, Fiſh Hooks and Lines, Doctors Vials, green, blue, and purple Spectacles, for preſerving weak Eyes, viſual Spectacles, of a new Conſtruction, by *Martin* the celebrated Optician, concave Spectacles and Hand Glaſſes for near-ſighted People, convex Spectacles and Glaſſes of all Sorts, Pocket Steelyards, Shoe Black and Breeches Ball, Smelling Bottles and Salts, Turners Tools of all Sorts, and ſome Hundreds of other uſeful Articles.

TRIANGULAR TRADE

Over time a shipping route also developed to bring colonists the slaves they needed. Ships full of goods such as cloth and weapons, sailed from England to Africa. In Africa the goods were exchanged for slaves. The ships then took the slaves to America.

When the slave ships arrived in America, colonists traded with the ship captains. They gave the captains items such as lumber, fish, and tobacco.

Slave traders kidnapped people from Africa and the Caribbean Islands. These people were then sold into slavery in America.

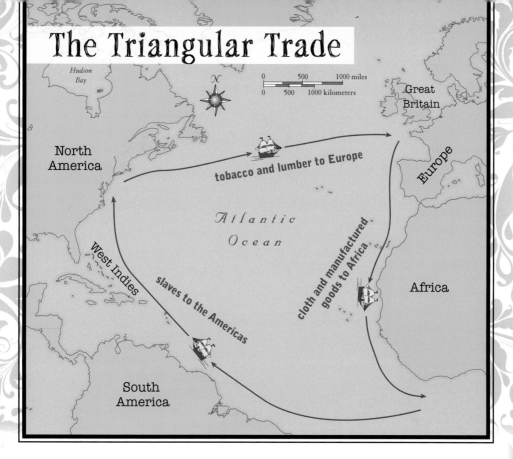

The Triangular Trade

Hudson Bay

0   500   1000 miles
0   500   1000 kilometers

Great Britain

North America

tobacco and lumber to Europe

Europe

Atlantic Ocean

West Indies

slaves to the Americas

cloth and manufactured goods to Africa

Africa

South America

In exchange, colonists got slaves. They also received supplies such as sugar and molasses that the ships had picked up in the **West Indies**. The American goods went to Great Britain for its people to use. Then the cycle started over.

Today we call this trade route the Triangular Trade. This trade changed the way colonists lived and worked. The Triangular Trade also changed the population. By 1750 as many as 200,000 slaves lived in the colonies.

West Indies—a group of islands that lie in waters south of present-day Florida

A MELTING POT OF FOODS

Colonists found life in the New World to be difficult, especially at first. But the European colonists soon adjusted to the land and the climate. They learned to hunt and farm. The colonists discovered what the American Indians already knew—that America offered a great variety of food.

a re-enactment of colonial foods

By the mid-1700s, the colonists had managed not only to survive but to thrive. But the colonists had not done it alone. American food still reflects the combination of three distinct groups—the European settlers, the American Indians, and the slaves.

Slaves learned to cook parts of the pig no one wanted. Many people eat ribs today because slaves figured out how to make them tasty. And we still eat some of the same foods colonists enjoyed. Next time you have beef jerky, pancakes, or pumpkin pie, think of the colonists and the American Indians. The foods people of the colonial period ate continue to shape our menus today.

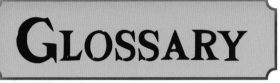

GLOSSARY

alcoholic (al-kuh-HOL-ik)—containing alcohol; alcohol is a colorless liquid found in drinks such as wine and beer

climate (KLY-muht)—the usual weather that occurs in a place

harvest (HAR-vist)—to collect or gather crops that are ripe

import (IM-port)—to bring goods into one country from another

merchant (MUR-chuhnt)—a person who buys and sells goods for profit

plantation (plan-TAY-shuhn)—a large farm; before 1865 plantations were run by slave labor

preserve (pri-ZURV)—to treat food so it does not spoil

ration (RASH-uhn)—a limited amount of something

venison (VEN-uh-suhn)—the meat of a deer

West Indies (WEST IN-deez)—a group of islands that lie in waters south of present-day Florida

READ MORE

Kalman, Bobbie. *A Visual Dictionary of a Colonial Community.* Crabtree Visual Dictionaries. New York: Crabtree Pub. Co., 2008.

Mara, Wil. *The Farmer.* Colonial People. New York: Marshall Cavendish Benchmark, 2010.

Raum, Elizabeth. *The Dreadful, Smelly Colonies: The Disgusting Details about Life During Colonial America.* Disgusting History. Mankato, Minn.: Capstone Press, 2010.

INTERNET SITES

FactHound offers a safe, fun way to find Internet sites related to this book. All of the sites on FactHound have been researched by our staff.

Here's all you do:

Visit *www.facthound.com*

Type in this code: 9781429664929

 Check out projects, games and lots more at **www.capstonekids.com**

INDEX

PRIMARY SOURCE BIBLIOGRAPHY

Page 23—a traditional churning song; first printed reference was found in *Satan's Invisible World Discovered* by George Sinclair (1684); a sound recording of a version of the song can be found on the Library of Congress American Memory site, call number AFS 4011A.

Page 25—as published in the *Virginia Gazette*, April 11, 1771.